My Little Cookbook

Discover a New Take on a Classical Italian Dish with these Delicious Lasagna Recipes

By
BookSumo Press

Published by
http://www.booksumo.com

LEGAL NOTES

Table of Contents

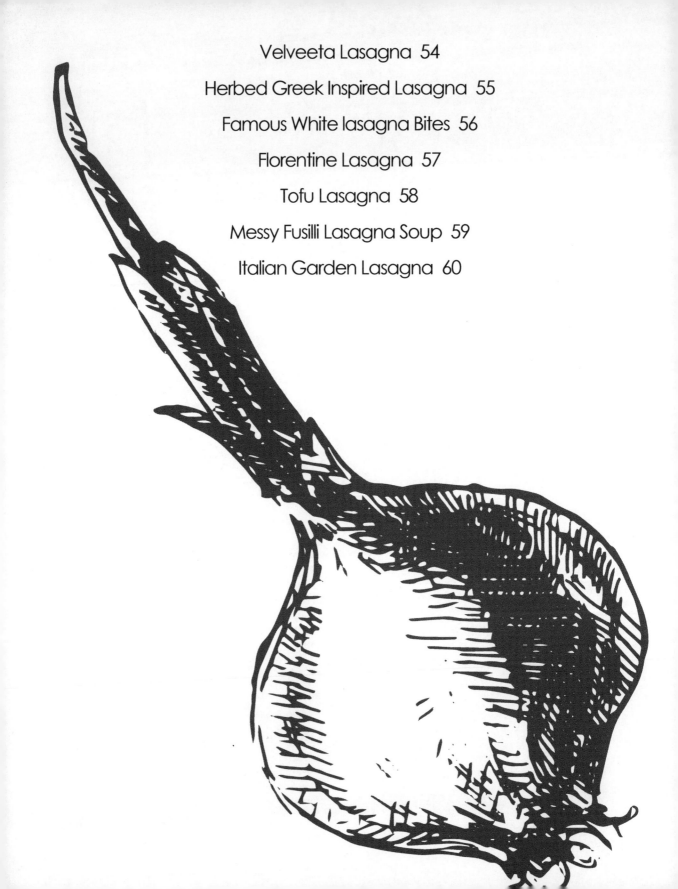

The Easiest
Lasagna

Prep Time: 20 mins
Total Time: 1 hr 35 mins

Servings per Recipe: 12

Calories	293 kcal
Carbohydrates	26.1 g
Cholesterol	61 mg
Fat	12.5 g
Protein	17.8 g
Sodium	514 mg

Ingredients

1 lb ground beef
2 1/2 C. Shredded Mozzarella Cheese
1 container Ricotta Cheese
1/2 C. Parmesan Cheese
1/4 C. chopped fresh parsley
1 egg, beaten
1 jar spaghetti sauce

1 C. water
12 lasagna noodles, uncooked

Directions

1. Set your oven to 350 degrees before doing anything else.
2. Get a bowl, mix: beaten eggs, 1 1/4 C. mozzarella, parsley, 1 /4 C. parmesan, and ricotta.
3. Fry your beef until brown, remove excess oils. Combine in your tomato sauce, with 1 C. of water that has been shaken in the pasta sauce jar. Combine everything smoothly.
4. Get your baking dish and layer: 1 C. of meat mix, lasagna noodles, 1/3 ricotta, continue until all ingredients used.
5. Cook for 1 hr with a covering of foil. 20 mins without.
6. Enjoy.

CLASSICAL
Lasagna

Prep Time: 30 mins
Total Time: 3 hrs 15 mins

Servings per Recipe: 12	
Calories	448 kcal
Carbohydrates	36.5 g
Cholesterol	82 mg
Fat	21.3 g
Protein	29.7 g
Sodium	1788 mg

Ingredients

1 lb sweet Italian sausage
3/4 lb lean ground beef
1/2 C. minced onion
2 cloves garlic, minced
1 can minced tomatoes
2 cans tomato paste
2 cans canned tomato sauce
1/2 C. water
2 tbsps white sugar
1 1/2 tsps dried basil leaves
1/2 tsp fennel seeds

1 tsp Italian seasoning
1 tbsp salt
1/4 tsp ground black pepper
4 tbsps chopped fresh parsley
12 lasagna noodles
16 oz ricotta cheese
1 egg
1/2 tsp salt
3/4 lb mozzarella cheese, sliced
3/4 C. grated Parmesan cheese

Directions

1. Get a small bowl, mix the following spices: 2 tbsps parsley, sugar, pepper, basil, 1 tbsp salt, Italian seasoning, and fennel seeds.
2. Get a heavy saucepan, cook the following until browned: garlic, sausage, onions, and beef. Then add the following, and let it simmer for 1.5 hours: water, minced tomatoes, tomato sauce, and paste, seasonings from your small bowl.
3. Set the oven to 375 degrees.
4. Boil lasagna noodles in a pot with salted water for 11 mins.
5. Get another small bowl, mix: .5 tsp of salt, parsley, beaten eggs, and ricotta.
6. Get your baking dish: Put 1.5 C. of sauce, 6 lasagna pieces, ricotta, and mozzarella. Continue this layering process until all of your noodles and sauce have been used. Add a final topping of parmesan (1/4 C.)
7. Spray some foil with nonstick spray and cover your baking dish. Cook for 25 mins covered, then another 25 mins uncovered. Let everything sit for 20 mins then enjoy.

Easier
Mexican Lasagna

🍲 Prep Time: 20 mins
🕐 Total Time: 1 hr 15 mins

Servings per Recipe: 1	
Calories	475 kcal
Carbohydrates	28.2 g
Cholesterol	97 mg
Fat	28.5 g
Protein	26.7 g
Sodium	1041 mg

Ingredients

2 lbs lean ground beef
2 (1.25 oz) packages taco seasoning mix
4 cloves garlic, minced
1/2 tsp cayenne pepper
1 tbsp chili powder
1/2 C. water
18 (6 inch) corn tortillas

1 (24 oz) jar salsa
1 C. sliced green onion
1 (16 oz) container sour cream
1 1/2 C. shredded Cheddar cheese
1 1/2 C. shredded Monterey Jack cheese

Directions

1. Set your oven to 375 degrees before doing anything else.
2. Fry your beef until no longer pink. Then remove excess oils and simmer for 12 mins with the following: water, taco seasoning, chili powder, cayenne, and garlic.
3. Get a baking dish and layer 6 tortillas, then 1/3 of the salsa, 1/2 of your beef, 1/2 of the onions, 1/2 of the sour cream (spread evenly overtop), and 1/2 of your Monterey and cheddar.
4. Continue making layers in this sequence until everything has been layered and the dish is full.
5. Cook for 45 mins. Let everything cool for 20 mins. Enjoy.

GARDEN
Lasagna I (Eggplant)

 Prep Time: 20 mins

Total Time: 1 hr 35 mins

Servings per Recipe: 12

Calories	404 kcal
Carbohydrates	30 g
Cholesterol	108 mg
Fat	20.6 g
Protein	27.7 g
Sodium	1496 mg

Ingredients

1 tsp olive oil for brushing
2 eggs
2 tbsps water
1 C. grated Parmesan cheese
1 C. Italian-seasoned breadcrumbs
salt and ground black pepper to taste
2 large eggplants, peeled and sliced into
1/2-inch rounds

2 tbsps olive oil
1 lb ground beef
48 oz chunky tomato sauce (such as Prego®)
2 C. shredded mozzarella cheese

Directions

1. Set your oven to 375 degrees before doing anything else.
2. Get 2 baking sheets and 1 dish. Coat each with 1 tsp of olive oil.
3. Get a bowl, mix: water and beaten eggs.
4. Get a 2nd bowl, mix: black pepper, parmesan, salt, and crumbled bread.
5. Dip eggplant pieces, into the first bowl, and then the 2nd. Lay them on the baking sheets and cook in the oven for 25 mins. Flip them and cook for 25 more mins. Set aside.
6. Set your oven temperature to 400 degrees before continuing.
7. Fry ground beef seasoned with pepper and salt in some olive oil until brown. Then remove any excess oils. Simmer the ground beef with tomato sauce for 3 mins. Set aside.
8. Layer the following in your baking dish: 1/3 eggplant, 1/3 beef, 1/3 mozzarella. Continue until the dish is full.
9. Cook everything in the oven for 15 mins.
10. Enjoy.

Garden
Lasagna II (Zucchini)

Prep Time: 15 mins
Total Time: 1 hr 25 mins

Servings per Recipe: 8
Calories   237 kcal
Carbohydrates   10.3 g
Cholesterol   71 mg
Fat   13.5 g
Protein   19.7 g
Sodium   550 mg

Ingredients

1 lb ground beef
1/2 C. chopped onion
1/2 C. chopped green bell pepper
1/4 C. finely chopped carrots
2 cloves garlic, minced
1 can tomato sauce
1/2 tsp dried oregano
1/2 tsp dried basil

salt and pepper to taste
5 zucchini
1 C. cottage cheese
1 egg, beaten
3/4 C. shredded mozzarella cheese
1/4 C. grated Parmesan cheese

Directions

1. Set your oven to 350 degrees before doing anything else. Then slice your zucchini into strips.

2. Get a bowl, mix: cottage cheese, and beaten eggs.

3. Fry your beef until browned. Remove any excess oils and season it with: pepper, oregano, salt, and basil. Add tomato sauce, onions, carrots, garlic, bell peppers. Lightly simmer everything for 12 mins.

4. Layer the following in a baking dish: 1/2 zucchini pieces, cottage cheese mix, 1/2 of your beef, 1/2 mozzarella, remaining zucchini, beef, and mozzarella. Finally some parmesan.

5. Cook in the oven for 45 to 50 mins.

6. Enjoy.

PEPPERONI
Lasagna

🥣 Prep Time: 30 mins
🕐 Total Time: 2 hrs 25 mins

Servings per Recipe: 12

Calories	545 kcal
Carbohydrates	27.6 g
Cholesterol	106 mg
Fat	33 g
Protein	36.8 g
Sodium	1997 mg

Ingredients

3/4 lb ground beef
1/2 lb salami, chopped
1/2 lb pepperoni sausage, chopped
1 onion, minced
2 (14.5 oz) cans stewed tomatoes
16 oz tomato sauce
6 oz tomato paste
1 tsp garlic powder
1 tsp dried oregano
1/2 tsp salt

1/4 tsp ground black pepper
9 lasagna noodles
4 C. shredded mozzarella cheese
2 C. cottage cheese
9 slices white American cheese
grated Parmesan cheese

Directions

1. Fry your pepperoni, beef, onions, and salami for 10 mins. Remove oil excess. Enter everything into your slow cooker on low with some pepper, tomato sauce and paste, salt, stewed tomatoes, oregano, and garlic powder for 2 hours.
2. Turn on your oven to 350 degrees before continuing.
3. Boil your lasagna in salt water until al dente for 10 mins, then remove all water.
4. In your baking dish, apply a light covering of sauce then layer: 1/3 noodles, 1 1/4 C. mozzarella, 2/3 C. cottage cheese, American cheese slices, 4 tsps parmesan, 1/3 meat. Continue until dish is full.
5. Cook for 30 mins.
6. Enjoy.

Spanish
Lasagna

Prep Time: 1 hr
Total Time: 2 hrs 45 mins

Servings per Recipe: 12

Calories	718 kcal
Carbohydrates	30.1 g
Cholesterol	186 mg
Fat	49.7 g
Protein	41.5 g
Sodium	1767 mg

Ingredients

4 C. canned minced tomatoes
1 (7 oz) can diced green chiles
1 (4 oz) can diced jalapeno peppers
1 onion, diced
3 cloves garlic, minced
10 sprigs fresh cilantro, chopped
2 tbsps ground cumin
2 lbs chorizo sausage

1 (32 oz) container ricotta cheese
4 eggs, lightly beaten
1 (16 oz) package Mexican style shredded four cheese blend
1 (8 oz) package no-cook lasagna noodles

Directions

1. Boil the following for 2 mins, then simmer on low for 55 mins: cilantro, tomatoes, cumin, green chilies, garlic, onion, and jalapenos.
2. Get a bowl, mix: beaten eggs, and ricotta.
3. Set your oven to 350 degrees before continuing.
4. Stir-fry your chorizos. Then remove oil excess and crumble the meat.
5. In your baking dish, apply a light covering of sauce then layer: sausage, 1/2 of your sauce, 1/2 shredded cheese, lasagna noodles, ricotta, more noodles, all remaining sauce, and more shredded cheese.
6. Coat some foil with nonstick spray, and cover the lasagna. Cook for 30 mins covered, and 15 mins without cover.
7. Enjoy.

HEALTHIER
Turkey Lasagna

Prep Time: 15 mins
Total Time: 1 hr 45 mins

Servings per Recipe: 8

Calories	263 kcal
Carbohydrates	24 g
Cholesterol	74 mg
Fat	9.2 g
Protein	25.4 g
Sodium	663 mg

Ingredients

1 (10 oz) package frozen chopped spinach, thawed and drained
1 C. low-fat cottage cheese
1 egg
cooking spray
1 onion, chopped
2 large garlic cloves, minced
2 C. chopped mushrooms
1 C. shredded carrots
1 lb ground turkey breast

1 (26 oz) jar low-fat pasta sauce (such as Healthy Request®)
1 C. water
1 tsp dried rosemary, minced
1 tsp dried oregano
1 tsp dried basil
6 no-boil lasagna noodles
1 C. shredded low-fat mozzarella cheese
1 C. tomato-vegetable juice cocktail

Directions

1. Set your oven to 400 degrees before doing anything else.
2. Coat a baking dish with nonstick spray.
3. With non-stick spray stir fry: carrots, onions, mushrooms, basil, rosemary, and oregano, and garlic for 5 mins. Combine in your turkey. Fry for another 5 mins. Finally add some water and tomato sauce. Lightly simmer for 10 mins.
4. Create the following layers: 1/3 of sauce, 1/2 lasagna noodles, 1/3 more of sauce, spinach, 1/2 mozzarella. Add rest of lasagna, veggie juice, and garnish with remaining mozzarella.
5. Cook for 45 mins, covered, with foil, then 10 mins without covering.
6. Enjoy.

Dessert
Lasagna

Prep Time: 15 mins
Total Time: 2 hrs 15 mins

Servings per Recipe: 12
Calories	321 kcal
Carbohydrates	62 g
Cholesterol	2 mg
Fat	4.7 g
Protein	4.7 g
Sodium	1266 mg

Ingredients

3 (3.4 oz) packages fat-free instant white chocolate pudding mix
3 C. skim milk
2 (8 oz) tubs fat-free whipped topping (such as Cool Whip®), divided

1 (14.4 oz) box chocolate graham crackers
1 (1.5 oz) chocolate candy bar cut into pieces

Directions

1. Get a bowl, mix until smooth: 1 container of whip topping, skim milk, and white chocolate pudding.
2. Get a baking dish and place graham crackers at the bottom. Layer 1/2 of your pudding then more graham crackers. Continue until dish is full. Garnish the final layer with minced candy bars.
3. Leave in the frig for 2-4 hours.
4. Enjoy.

NO-NOODLE
Lasagna

Prep Time: 20 mins
Total Time: 45 mins

Servings per Recipe: 12
Calories	461 kcal
Carbohydrates	35.3 g
Cholesterol	118 mg
Fat	20.3 g
Protein	32 g
Sodium	975 mg

Ingredients

1 lb ground beef
1 (26 oz) jar spaghetti sauce
1/2 tsp garlic powder
3 C. cooked rice, cooled
2 eggs, lightly beaten
3/4 C. shredded Parmesan cheese,
divided

2 1/4 C. shredded mozzarella cheese
2 C. cottage cheese

Directions

1. Set your oven to 375 degrees before doing anything else.
2. Fry your beef until browned for 8 mins, and remove excess grease. Combine in your tomato sauce and also garlic powder.
3. Get a bowl, mix: 1/4 C. parmesan, whisked eggs, and rice.
4. Get a 2nd bowl, mix: 1/4 C. parmesan, cottage cheese, and 2 C. mozzarella
5. Layer the following in a dish: 1/2 rice, 1/2 cheese mix, 1/2 meat. Continue until dish is full. Then top with more mozzarella.
6. Cook for 25 mins, until sauce is simmering, and cheese melted.

No-Bake
3 Cheese Lasagna

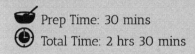 Prep Time: 30 mins

Total Time: 2 hrs 30 mins

Servings per Recipe: 10

Calories	521 kcal
Carbohydrates	50.3 g
Cholesterol	110 mg
Fat	20.6 g
Protein	33.1 g
Sodium	861 mg

Ingredients

1 (16 oz) package lasagna noodles
1 lb lean ground beef
1 1/2 (26 oz) jars spaghetti sauce
2 C. shredded mozzarella cheese
1/2 C. grated Parmesan cheese

1 (8 oz) container ricotta cheese
2 eggs
2 C. shredded mozzarella cheese

Directions

1. Boil lasagna in salted water for 7 min until al dente. Remove all water.
2. Fry your beef until brown, remove oil excess, mix in tomato sauce, simmer for 5 mins. Turn off heat.
3. Get a bowl, mix: beaten eggs, 2 C. mozzarella, ricotta, and parmesan.
4. Place half of your beef into the slow cooker first, then some lasagna noodles. Then 1/4 of the cheese mix, then 1/4 more sauce. Continue adding layers until nothing is lest. Topmost layer should be 2 C. of mozzarella.
5. Set slow cooker to high for 3 hours. Then set heat to low for 8 hours.
6. Enjoy.

GARDEN
Lasagna III (Broccoli, Carrots, & Corn)

 Prep Time: 30 mins
Total Time: 1 hr 10 mins

Servings per Recipe: 10
Calories	534 kcal
Carbohydrates	48.8 g
Cholesterol	103 mg
Fat	27 g
Protein	26.6 g
Sodium	1091 mg

Ingredients

1 box lasagna noodles
2 eggs, beaten
1 box part-skim ricotta cheese
2 cans condensed cream of mushroom soup
2 C. shredded Cheddar cheese
1 C. grated Parmesan cheese

1 C. sour cream
1 package herb and garlic soup mix
1 bag chopped frozen broccoli, thawed
1 bag frozen sliced carrots
1 bag frozen corn kernels

Directions

1. Set your oven to 375 degrees before anything else.
2. Boil noodles in water with salt for 10 mins. Remove all water, set aside.
3. Get a bowl, mix: soup mix, beaten eggs, sour cream, ricotta, parmesan, cheddar, and mushroom soup.
4. In your baking layer everything in the following manner: lasagna, cheese mix, carrots, corn, broccoli. Continue until all ingredients used. Cheese should be upmost layer.
5. Cook for 30, with a cover of foil. 10 mins without.
6. Enjoy.

Pretty
Easy Lasagna

Prep Time: 15 mins
Total Time: 40 mins

Servings per Recipe: 8
Calories	386 kcal
Carbohydrates	29.6 g
Cholesterol	46 mg
Fat	19.3 g
Protein	22.1 g
Sodium	1135 mg

Ingredients

2 C. uncooked penne pasta
1 lb ground Italian sausage
1 (26 oz) jar spaghetti sauce

1 C. cottage cheese
2 C. shredded mozzarella cheese, divided

Directions

1. Set your oven to 350 degrees before doing anything else.
2. Boil your pasta for 8 mins in water and salt. While stir frying your Italian sausage for 10 mins. Then remove oil excesses. Combine pasta, and tomato sauce, with your sausage. And simmer the mix for 3 mins.
3. Now coat a baking dish with nonstick spray. And layer 1/2 of the sauce and pasta at the bottom. Add a layer of cottage cheese, 1/2 mozzarella, add the rest of the pasta. Finally add the rest of the mozzarella.
4. Bake for 30 mins covered with foil. 5 mins without a covering.
5. Enjoy.

MICROWAVE
Mexican Lasagna

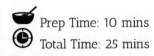

Prep Time: 10 mins
Total Time: 25 mins

Servings per Recipe: 10
Calories   709 kcal
Carbohydrates   35.8 g
Cholesterol   143 mg
Fat   45.4 g
Protein   39.3 g
Sodium   1304 mg

Ingredients

11 oz lasagna noodles
1 lb lean ground beef
24 oz tomato sauce
1/2 C. water
1 (1 oz) package taco seasoning mix

8 C. shredded Cheddar cheese
1/2 C. minced tortilla chips

Directions

1. Boil your pasta for 10 mins in water and salt. Remove all water. Set aside.
2. Fry your beef until browned, and remove excess oils. Combine in some taco seasoning, then tomato and finally water. Lightly simmer for 6 mins.
3. Get your dish (must be able to fit in microwave), and layer in the following manner: lasagna noodles, beef mix, cheese. Continue until dish is full.
4. Microwave for 10 mins on the highest power setting covered with plastic wrap.
5. Garnish with tortilla chips.
6. Enjoy.

Easy
Cheddar Lasagna

🥣 Prep Time: 30 mins
🕐 Total Time: 1 hr

Servings per Recipe: 1
Calories	643 kcal
Carbohydrates	53.4 g
Cholesterol	108 mg
Fat	29.3 g
Protein	41.3 g
Sodium	707 mg

Ingredients

1 (16 oz) package lasagna noodles
1 lb lean ground beef
salt and pepper to taste
1 (16 oz) jar spaghetti sauce
1 clove garlic, minced

1/2 lb shredded mozzarella cheese
1/2 lb shredded Cheddar cheese
1 pint ricotta cheese

Directions

1. Set your oven to 350 degrees before doing anything else.
2. Get a bowl mix: ricotta, mozzarella, and cheddar.
3. Boil your noodles in water and salt for 9 mins. Remove water. Set aside
4. Fry your beef seasoned with pepper and salt, until cooked. Remove oil excess. Combine in garlic and tomato sauce. Simmer for 6 mins.
5. In your baking dish layer: noodles, meat, and then cheese. Continue until dish is full.
6. Cook for 30 mins.
7. Enjoy.

CUPCAKE
Lasagnas

Prep Time: 15 mins
Total Time: 35 mins

Servings per Recipe: 12
Calories   147 kcal
Carbohydrates   16.8 g
Cholesterol   17 mg
Fat   5.5 g
Protein   7.1 g
Sodium   445 mg

Ingredients

nonstick spray
1 C. shredded mozzarella cheese
1 C. grated Asiago cheese

2 C. prepared pasta sauce
1/2 (16 oz) package wonton wrappers

Directions

1. Set your oven to 375 degrees before doing anything else.
2. Coat muffin tins with some nonstick spray.
3. Get a bowl, mix: Asiago and mozzarella.
4. Take your muffin tin and in each section put a wonton wrap.
5. Fill each section halfway with sauce, then 2 and half tbsps of cheese, then add a new wonton wrap to each. Add sauce, and more cheese.
6. Cook for 25 mins.
7. Enjoy.

Stovetop
Lasagna

🥘 Prep Time: 10 mins
🕐 Total Time: 45 mins

Servings per Recipe: 4
Calories	441 kcal
Carbohydrates	48.8 g
Cholesterol	69 mg
Fat	15.8 g
Protein	27.2 g
Sodium	1148 mg

Ingredients

1 lb ground beef
4 C. water
3 beef bouillon cubes
7 dry lasagna noodles, split in half
1 (10.75 oz) can condensed tomato soup
1 onion, chopped
2 cloves garlic, minced

1 1/2 tbsps Italian seasoning
1/2 tsp ground black pepper
1 tsp cornstarch
salt to taste

Directions

1. Fry your beef for 10 mins and remove oils. Combine in some bouillon cubes, and water. Stir until cubes dissolve.

2. Then bring everything to a boiling state. Put in noodles and the following: pepper, tomato soup, Italian seasoning, garlic, and onions. Lower the heat and simmer for 12 mins.

3. Get a bowl and mix some cornstarch with one C. of sauce, then combine it back with the noodles. Simmer for another 3 to 5 mins.

4. Enjoy after everything cools.

LASAGNA
Alfredo

Prep Time: 35 mins
Total Time: 1 hr 30 mins

Servings per Recipe: 8
Calories	712 kcal
Carbohydrates	53.7 g
Cholesterol	98 mg
Fat	40.4 g
Protein	36.6 g
Sodium	1071 mg

Ingredients

1 (16 oz) package lasagna noodles
2 tbsps olive oil
1 small onion, chopped
1 (16 oz) package frozen chopped
spinach, thawed
7 oz basil pesto
30 oz ricotta cheese
1 egg
1/2 tsp salt

1/4 tsp ground black pepper
1/4 tsp ground nutmeg
2 C. mozzarella cheese, shredded
9 oz Alfredo-style pasta sauce
1/4 C. grated Parmesan cheese

Directions

1. Set your oven to 350 degrees before doing anything else.
2. Coat your baking dish with nonstick spray, or oil.
3. Get a bowl, mix: whisked eggs, nutmeg, pepper, ricotta, and salt.
4. Boil your pasta for 9 mins in salty water. Remove all liquid.
5. Stir fry spinach and onions with olive oil. Until onions are soft. Turn off the heat then add in pesto.
6. Add everything to a dish in the following manner: noodles, spinach, ricotta, mozzarella. Continue until everything is used. Garnish with some parmesan.
7. Cook for 50 mins. While covered. Let everything sit for 10 mins.
8. Enjoy.

Garden
Lasagna III (Asparagus)

Prep Time: 20 mins
Total Time: 30 mins

Servings per Recipe: 4
Calories	388 kcal
Carbohydrates	33.2 g
Cholesterol	44 mg
Fat	18.8 g
Protein	22.6 g
Sodium	1008 mg

Ingredients

5 lasagna noodles, halved
2 tbsps margarine
2 cloves garlic, chopped
2 tbsps all-purpose flour
1 1/2 C. milk
1/2 tsp dried thyme
1 (15 oz) can asparagus, drained

1 C. julienned fully cooked ham
1 C. shredded mozzarella cheese

Directions

1. Boil your noodles for 9 mins in water and salt. Remove all water. Set aside.
2. Stir fry your onions in melted butter, then add some flour and thyme. Continue stirring until everything is even and smooth.
3. Add milk, and continue stirring. Lower heat and simmer for 10 mins until everything becomes sauce like. Set aside.
4. Coat a baking dish (which can fit in the microwave) with nonstick spray or oil. Enter in your noodles, then some sauce, ham, asparagus, and mozzarella. Continue layering in this process until dish is full or all ingredients used.
5. For 10 mins microwave the lasagna covered with plastic. Increase the time if the cheese is not melted after 10 mins.
6. Enjoy.

MAGGIE'S
Favorite Lasagna

Prep Time: 10 mins
Total Time: 1 hr 10 mins

Servings per Recipe: 6
Calories	609 kcal
Carbohydrates	49.4 g
Cholesterol	175 mg
Fat	28.5 g
Protein	39.6 g
Sodium	1025 mg

Ingredients

2 C. ricotta cheese
1 (10 oz) package frozen chopped spinach - thawed, drained and squeezed dry
1 1/2 C. grated Romano cheese
2 eggs
salt and pepper to taste

1/4 C. spaghetti sauce
1 (25 oz) package frozen cheese ravioli
1/2 C. spaghetti sauce
1/2 C. grated Romano cheese

Directions

1. Set your oven to 375 degrees before doing anything else.
2. Get a bowl, mix: pepper, ricotta, salt, spinach, 1.5 C. Romano, and whisked eggs.
3. Coat a dish with nonstick spray.
4. Layer the following in your dish: 1/4 C. sauce, raviolis, 1 C. ricotta. Continue until dish is full. Add a topping of Romano.
5. Cook for 40 mins covered with foil in the oven. Finally remove the foil and continue baking for 10 more mins.
6. Enjoy.

Pesto
Lasagna

Prep Time: 25 mins
Total Time: 1 hr 31 mins

Servings per Recipe: 8
Calories	675 kcal
Fat	38.4 g
Carbohydrates	38.3g
Protein	46.5 g
Cholesterol	118 mg
Sodium	887 mg

Ingredients

1/4 C. pine nuts
3 C. fresh basil leaves
3/4 C. grated Parmesan cheese
1/2 C. olive oil
4 cloves garlic
12 lasagna noodles
cooking spray
3 tbsps olive oil
1 C. chopped onion
3 cloves garlic, crushed

2 (12 oz.) packages frozen chopped spinach
3 C. diced cooked chicken breast
1 tsp salt
1 tsp ground black pepper
2 C. ricotta cheese
3/4 C. grated Parmesan cheese
1 egg
2 C. shredded mozzarella cheese

Directions

1. Set your oven to 350 degrees F before doing anything else and coat a 13x9-inch casserole dish with some cooking spray.
2. In a heated nonstick skillet, add the pine nuts on medium heat and cook, stirring often for about 3 minutes or till toasted.
3. In a food processor, add the toasted pine nuts and the remaining pesto ingredients and pulse till smooth and keep aside.
4. For the lasagna, in a large pan of lightly salted boiling water, add the lasagna noodles and cook them for about 8-10 minutes or till desired doneness and drain well and keep aside.
5. In a large skillet, heat oil on medium-high heat and sauté the onion and garlic for about 5 minutes.
6. Add the spinach and cook for about 5 minutes.
7. Add the chicken and cook for about 5 minutes and stir in some salt and black pepper and remove from heat and let it cool.
8. In a bowl, mix together parmesan, ricotta, egg, 1 1/2 C. of pesto and chicken mixture.

9. Place the remaining pesto in the bottom of the prepared casserole dish evenly and top everything with 4 lasagna noodles.

10. Place one-third of the chicken mixture over the noodles evenly and followed by one-third of the mozzarella and repeat the layers twice.

11. Cook everything in the oven for about 35-40 minutes or till the top becomes golden brown and bubbly.

Lasagna
Bakes

🥣 Prep Time: 40 mins
🕐 Total Time: 1 hr 40 mins

Servings per Recipe: 4
Calories	637 kcal
Fat	21.6 g
Carbohydrates	70.1g
Protein	44.3 g
Cholesterol	87 mg
Sodium	1281 mg

Ingredients

8 whole wheat lasagna noodles
1/2 lb ground turkey
6 cloves garlic, crushed
1 (10 oz.) package frozen diced spinach, thawed and drained
1/2 C. diced fresh chives
1/2 tsp dried oregano
1/2 tsp dried parsley
1/4 tsp dried basil

2 egg whites
1 (15 oz.) container reduced-fat ricotta cheese
2 tbsps crumbled low-fat feta cheese
2 tbsps grated Parmesan cheese
1/2 tsp ground black pepper
1 (28 oz.) jar low-fat tomato pasta sauce
1/2 C. shredded low-fat Cheddar cheese

Directions

1. Set your oven to 375 degrees before doing anything else.
2. Boil your pasta in water and salt for 9 mins then remove all the liquids.
3. Begin to stir fry your garlic and turkey for 12 mins and break the meat into pieces as it cooks.
4. Once the meat is fully done add in: the basil, spinach, parsley, oregano, and chives.
5. Stir the mix and cook everything for 60 more secs then shut the heat.
6. Get a bowl, combine: parmesan, egg whites, feta, and ricotta. Stir the mix then add in the black pepper and turkey mix.
7. On a working surface place a large piece of wax paper and lay out the pasta.
8. Form your cheese mix into eight balls and put one ball on each piece of lasagna and roll everything up into a burrito shape. Continue this process with all of your noodles.
9. Now coat the bottom of a casserole dish with tomato sauce and then layer your lasagna rolls over the sauce with seam portion facing downwards in the sauce.
10. Top the rolls with the rest of the pasta sauce and a layering of cheddar.
11. Place a covering of foil around the dish and put everything in oven for 45 mins. Enjoy.

CLASSICAL
Lasagna II

Prep Time: 30 mins
Total Time: 2 hrs

Servings per Recipe: 8
Calories	664 kcal
Fat	29.5 g
Carbohydrates	48.3g
Protein	50.9 g
Cholesterol	1168 mg
Sodium	1900 mg

Ingredients

1 1/2 lbs lean ground beef
1 onion, diced
2 cloves garlic, minced
1 tbsp diced fresh basil
1 tsp dried oregano
2 tbsps brown sugar
1 1/2 tsps salt
1 (29 oz.) can diced tomatoes
2 (6 oz.) cans tomato paste

12 dry lasagna noodles
2 eggs, beaten
1 pint part-skim ricotta cheese
1/2 C. grated Parmesan cheese
2 tbsps dried parsley
1 tsp salt
1 lb mozzarella cheese, shredded
2 tbsps grated Parmesan cheese

Directions

1. Stir fry your garlic, onions, and beef for 3 mins then combine in: tomato paste, basil, diced tomatoes, oregano, 1.5 tsp salt, and brown sugar.
2. Now set your oven to 375 degrees before doing anything else.
3. Begin to boil your pasta in water and salt for 9 mins then remove all the liquids.
4. Get a bowl, combine: 1 tsp salt, eggs, parsley, ricotta, and parmesan.
5. Place a third of the pasta in a casserole dish and top everything with half of the cheese mix, one third of the sauce, and 1/2 of the mozzarella.
6. Continue layering in this manner until all the ingredients have been used up.
7. Then top everything with some more parmesan.
8. Cook the lasagna in the oven for 35 mins.
9. Enjoy.

Cajun
Lasagna

🍲 Prep Time: 15 mins
🕐 Total Time: 1 hr 45 mins

Servings per Recipe: 12
Calories   488 kcal
Fat   29 g
Carbohydrates   32g
Protein   25.4 g
Cholesterol   75 mg
Sodium   1045 mg

Ingredients

1 (16 oz.) package lasagna noodles
1 lb andouille sausage, quartered lengthwise and sliced
1 lb skinless, boneless chicken breast halves, cut into chunks
2 tsps Cajun seasoning
1 tsp dried sage
1/2 C. chopped onion

1/2 C. chopped celery
1/4 C. chopped red bell pepper
1 tbsp finely chopped garlic
2 (10 oz.) containers Alfredo Sauce, divided
1 1/2 C. shredded mozzarella cheese
1/2 C. grated Parmesan cheese

Directions

1. Set your oven to 325 degrees before doing anything else.
2. Get your pasta boiling in water and salt for 9 mins then remove all the liquids.
3. Begin to fry your chicken and sausage then top the meats with the sage and Cajun spice.
4. Continue cooking the meat until the chicken is fully done for 10 mins.
5. Place everything to the side then begin to stir fry your garlic, onions, bell peppers, and celery until everything is soft.
6. Place these veggies to the side as well.
7. Combine the meat and veggies together then add in 1 jar of Alfredo and stir everything evenly.
8. Coat a casserole dish with oil then lay in 4 pieces of pasta.
9. Top the pasta with half of the Alfredo mix.
10. Continue layering in this manner until all the pasta has been added.
11. Top the layers with the remaining jar of sauce then layer your parmesan and mozzarella over everything.
12. Cook the lasagna in the oven for 60 mins. Enjoy.

CHEESY
Beef Lasagna

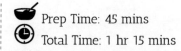

Prep Time: 45 mins
Total Time: 1 hr 15 mins

Servings per Recipe: 6
Calories	697.7
Cholesterol	165.8mg
Sodium	1693.2mg
Carbohydrates	58.6g
Protein	44.9g

Ingredients

12 oz. lasagna noodles
2 tbsps salad oil
2 garlic cloves, diced
1 medium onion, chopped
1 lb ground beef
1 1/2 tsps salt
1/4 tsp pepper
1/2 tsp rosemary or 1/2 tsp basil
1 tbsp parsley, diced

12 oz. tomato paste
1 1/2 C. hot water
2 eggs, beaten
1 pint cottage cheese or 1/2 lb ricotta cheese
1/2 lb mozzarella cheese, sliced
1/4 C. parmesan cheese, grated

Directions

1. Set your oven to 350 degrees F before doing anything else.
2. In a pan of salted boiling water, cook the lasagna noodles for about 15 minutes or till tender and drain well.
3. In a skillet, heat salad oil on medium heat and sauté the onion and garlic till soft.
4. Add the beef with seasoning and cook till crumbly then stir in the hot water and tomato paste.
5. Cook everything for about 5 minutes.
6. In a bowl, add the ricotta, cottage cheese and eggs and beat till well combined.
7. In a 13x9-inch baking dish, spread a thin layer of meat mixture evenly.
8. Place half of the lasagna noodles over the sauce followed by all of the egg-cheese mixture and half of the mozzarella.
9. Now spread half of the remaining meat mixture, followed by the remaining noodles, remaining meat mixture and remaining mozzarella and then top with Parmesan.
10. Cook the mix in the oven for about 30 minutes.

Eastern
European Style Lasagna

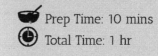 Prep Time: 10 mins
Total Time: 1 hr

Servings per Recipe: 12

Calories	303 kcal
Fat	17.6 g
Carbohydrates	22.1g
Protein	14.4 g
Cholesterol	42 mg
Sodium	1115 mg

Ingredients

9 lasagna noodles
1 (10.75 oz.) can condensed cream of mushroom soup
1 (10.75 oz.) can condensed cream of chicken soup

2 C. milk
1 lb kielbasa, cut in half, diced
1 (20 oz.) can sauerkraut, drained
8 oz. shredded mozzarella cheese

Directions

1. Set your oven to 375 degrees before doing anything else.
2. Boil your pasta in water and salt for 9 mins. Then remove all the liquids.
3. Now blend until smooth: milk, chicken soup, and mushrooms.
4. Layer the following in a casserole dish: 3 noodles, 1 C. soup, half sauerkraut, half of your sausage, and half of the cheese.
5. Continue layering until all of the ingredients have been used.
6. End with noodles if possible.
7. Now place a covering of foil around the dish and cook everything in the oven for 30 mins.
8. Take off the foil and continue cooking the contents for 20 more mins.
9. Now top everything with some cheese and let it melt outside the oven.
10. Enjoy.

SQUASH
Lasagna

Prep Time: 30 mins
Total Time: 1 hr 45 mins

Servings per Recipe: 6
Calories	280 kcal
Fat	15.9 g
Carbohydrates	24.5g
Protein	14.1 g
Cholesterol	27 mg
Sodium	1294 mg

Ingredients

1 spaghetti squash, halved lengthwise
and seeded
1 onion, chopped
2 tbsps minced garlic
2 (14 oz.) cans stewed tomatoes
1 tbsp dried basil
1 cube vegetable bouillon

black pepper to taste
1 (15 oz.) can black olives, chopped
1 C. shredded mozzarella cheese
1 C. shredded Parmesan cheese

Directions

1. Coat a casserole dish with non-stick spray and then set your oven to 325 degrees before doing anything else.
2. Cook the squash in the oven for 37 mins then take everything out of the oven.
3. Shred the flesh and place it in a bowl. But keep the rinds as well separate.
4. Stir fry your garlic and onions in a pan with nonstick spray until browned and then add in: black pepper, tomatoes, bouillon, and basil.
5. Let this cook for 17 mins.
6. Layer the following in the squash rinds: tbsp of tomatoes mix, squash, mozzarella, olive.
7. Continue layering until all the rinds are full. Now top with some parmesan.
8. Once all your ingredients have been layered cook everything in the oven for 22 mins.
9. Enjoy.

Vidalia
Potato and Noodles Pierogi Bake

Prep Time: 10 mins
Total Time: 30 mins

Servings per Recipe: 4
Calories	579.0
Fat	28.8g
Cholesterol	122.8mg
Sodium	764.2mg
Carbohydrates	58.5g
Protein	21.7g

Ingredients

1/2 lb wide egg noodles, cooked
1/4 C. butter
1 1/2 C. mashed potatoes, prepared
5 slices American cheese
1/2 C. cheddar cheese, shredded

1/2 C. mozzarella cheese, shredded
1/4 large Vidalia onion, minced
2 garlic cloves, minced
salt and pepper, to taste

Directions

1. Before you do anything, preheat the oven to 350 F. Grease a casserole dish with a cooking spray.
2. Prepare the noodles by following the instructions on the package.
3. Place a large pan over medium heat: Heat in it the butter. Cook in it the garlic with onion, a pinch of salt and pepper.
4. Cook them for 5 min. Spread half of the lasagna sheets in the greased dish.
5. Spread over it half of the cheese followed by all the potato. Season them with some salt and pepper.
6. Cover it with the remaining pasta and cheese. Dot it with butter then bake it for 12 min.
7. Allow the lasagna casserole to rest for 5 min then serve it.
8. Enjoy.

CEDARS
of Lebanon Lasagna

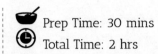

Prep Time: 30 mins
Total Time: 2 hrs

Servings per Recipe: 10
Calories	699.0
Fat	40.4g
Cholesterol	131.3mg
Sodium	662.2mg
Carbohydrates	44.3g
Protein	39.1g

Ingredients

1 (16 oz.) packages elbow macaroni
1/4 C. butter
1 lb sharp cheddar cheese, cut into cubes divided
1 C. parmesan cheese
1 medium onion, chopped
2 garlic cloves, minced
1 tbsp oil
1 small celery rib, chopped
1 green bell pepper, cut into strips
2 lb. ground chuck

1 tsp chili powder
1/4 tsp cumin
1 dash oregano
8 mushrooms, thinly sliced
1 dash Worcestershire sauce
salt and pepper
red pepper flakes
2 (16 oz.) cans chopped tomatoes
1 (8 oz.) cans tomato sauce

Directions

1. Set your oven to 350 degrees F before doing anything else. In a large pan of the lightly salted boiling water, prepare the macaroni according to the package's directions. Drain well.
2. For the sauce in a pan, heat the oil on medium heat and sauté the onion and garlic till browned. Add the celery and green pepper and cook till softened.
3. Transfer the onion mixture into a bowl.
4. In the same pan, add the ground beef and cook till browned completely.
5. Add the onion mixture, salt, pepper, chili powder, cumin, Worcestershire sauce, pinch oregano, mushrooms, red pepper flakes, tomatoes and tomato sauce and stir to combine.
6. Reduce the heat to low and simmer for about 1 hour. In a large casserole dish, place a layer of the cooked macaroni and dot with the butter, followed by add 1/2 of the cheese cubes, a layer of the sauce and sprinkle with the red pepper flakes.
7. Repeat the layers, finishing with the sauce; and sprinkle with the Parmesan cheese.
8. Cook in the oven for about 30 minutes.

Roasted
Veggies Lasagna

Prep Time: 35 mins
Total Time: 1 hr 20 mins

Servings per Recipe: 10

Calories	410 kcal
Fat	14.6 g
Carbohydrates	48.4g
Protein	22.2 g
Cholesterol	38 mg
Sodium	1184 mg

Ingredients

olive oil cooking spray
2 zucchini, sliced
2 green bell peppers, cut in 1-inch pieces
1 (8 oz) package sliced fresh mushrooms
1 onion, cut into 8 wedges
1 tbsp chopped fresh basil
1 clove garlic, pressed
1/2 tsp salt

1/4 tsp ground black pepper
12 lasagna noodles
2 (28 oz) jars pasta sauce
1 (16 oz) package shredded mozzarella cheese
1 C. freshly shredded Parmesan cheese

Directions

1. Before you do anything set the oven to 400 F. Grease a casserole dish. Place it aside. Lay the zucchini, bell peppers, mushrooms, and onion wedges on the baking pan.
2. Top them with the garlic and basil then grease them with a cooking spray.
3. Sprinkle some salt with pepper on top. Cook them in the oven for 24 min.
4. Cook the lasagna noodles according to the instructions on the package until they become dente.
5. Remove them from the water and place them aside. Place a heavy saucepan over medium heat. Add to it the pasta sauce and bring to a simmer.
6. Get a mixing bowl: Stir in it the parmesan and mozzarella cheese. Place it aside. Spread 1/3 C. of pasta sauce in the greased casserole dish.
7. Top it with 3 lasagna noodles, 1/4 C. of the roasted veggies, 1/4 of the sauce and 1/4 C. of the cheese mix.
8. Repeat the process to make another 3 layers with cheese on top. Cook the lasagna in the oven for 24 min then serve it warm.
9. Enjoy.

BACKWOODS
Lasagna

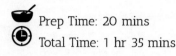

Prep Time: 20 mins
Total Time: 1 hr 35 mins

Servings per Recipe: 12
Calories	351.7
Fat	14.1g
Cholesterol	53.1mg
Sodium	599.6mg
Carbohydrates	31.4g
Protein	23.0g

Ingredients

1 (16 oz) packages lasagna noodles
1 lb andouille sausage, quartered length wise and sliced
1 lb boneless skinless chicken breast half, cut into chunks
2 tsp cajun seasoning
1 tsp dried sage
1/2 C. chopped onion
1/2 C. chopped celery

1/4 C. chopped red bell pepper
1 tbsp finely chopped garlic
2 (10 oz) containers alfredo sauce, divided
1/2 C. shredded mozzarella cheese
1/2 C. grated parmesan cheese
salt

Directions

1. Before you do anything, preheat the oven to 325 F.
2. Prepare the pasta by following the instructions on the package cooking for 8 min only. Drain it and place it aside.
3. Place a pan over medium heat. Cook in it the sausage, chicken, Cajun seasoning and sage for 10 min. Drain them and place them aside.
4. Add the onion, celery, bell pepper and garlic to the pan. Cook them for 7 min. Stir in the cooked chicken mix with 10 oz of Alfredo sauce.
5. Lay 4 pasta noodles in the bottom of a greased glass baking dish. Pour over it 1/2 of the chicken mix. Drizzle over it half of the remaining Alfredo sauce.
6. Repeat the process to make another layer. Top them with the mozzarella and parmesan cheese. Place the casserole in the oven and cook it for 1 h.
7. Once the time is up, serve your lasagna hot.
8. Enjoy.

Lasagna
Crepes

Prep Time: 40 mins
Total Time: 1 hr 40 mins

Servings per Recipe: 6

Calories	848.4
Fat	41.5g
Cholesterol	268.5mg
Sodium	1828.6mg
Carbohydrates	77.0g
Protein	40.0g

Ingredients

Crepes
3 eggs
1 C. water
1 1/2 C. all-purpose flour
nonstick Pam cooking spray
Filling
2 lb. whole milk ricotta cheese
1/2 C. Pecorino Romano cheese, freshly grated
1 C. shredded whole milk mozzarella
3 tbsp. fresh basil, chopped

4 tbsp. fresh parsley, chopped
2 eggs, beaten
1/2 tsp. fresh ground pepper
Other
2 quarts marinara sauce
1 C. shredded mozzarella cheese

Directions

1. For the crepes: in a bowl, add the water and eggs and beat well.
2. Slowly, add the flour and beat until smooth.
3. Place in the fridge for about 30 minutes.
4. Meanwhile, for the filling: in a bowl, add the eggs, Ricotta, Mozzarella, Pecorino Romano cheese, parsley, basil and pepper and mix until well combined.
5. Cover the bowl and place in the fridge for about 30 minutes.
6. Place about 1/3 C. of the mixture and tilt the pan to spread in a thin layer.
7. Cook for about 1 minute.
8. Flip and cook for about 5 seconds more.
9. Repeat with the remaining mixture.
10. Transfer the crepes onto a smooth surface and let them cool.
11. Set your oven to 325 degrees F.
12. Place 2 tbsp. of the filling mixture onto the center of each crepe.

13. Carefully, roll each crepe.
14. In the bottom of a 13x9-inch baking dish, place a layer of the marinara sauce and arrange 1 layer of the crepes on top, seam side down.
15. Repeat the layers, ending with a layer of the marinara sauce.
16. With a piece of the foil, cover the baking dish and cook in the oven for about 40 minutes.
17. Remove the foil and top with the remaining Mozzarella cheese evenly.
18. Cook in the oven for about 5-10 minutes.
19. Remove from the oven and keep aside for about 9-10 minutes.
20. Enjoy.

Katrina's
Mesa Lasagna

Prep Time: 20 mins
Total Time: 50 mins

Servings per Recipe: 4
Calories   1154.6
Fat   44.8g
Cholesterol   103.9mg
Sodium   3411.2mg
Carbohydrates   139.7g
Protein   49.7g

Ingredients

1 lb ground beef round
1/2 C. chopped green pepper
1/2 C. chopped onion
2/3 C. water
1 envelopes taco seasoning
1 cans black beans
1 cans petite diced tomatoes

6 large flour tortillas
1 cans refried beans
3-4 C. Mexican blend cheese
chopped fresh cilantro leaves
sour cream

Directions

1. Before you do anything, preheat the oven to 350 F. Grease a casserole dish.
2. Place a large pan over medium heat. Cook in it the beef with onion and green pepper for 8 min.
3. Stir in the water with taco seasoning. Cook them until they start boiling. Lower the heat and let them cook for an extra 6 min.
4. Add the tomatoes and black beans. Cook them for 12 min.
5. Lay 2 tortillas in the bottom of the casserole. Top it with half of the refried beans followed by half of the beef mixture, and 1 C. of shredded cheese.
6. Repeat the process to make another layer. Cover the second layer with the remaining tortillas and cheese.
7. Use a piece of foil to cover the casserole. Cook it in the oven for 32 min. serve it warm with your favorite toppings.
8. Enjoy.

EVELINE'S
Latin Lasagna

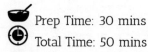

Prep Time: 30 mins
Total Time: 50 mins

Servings per Recipe: 4

Calories	1075.4
Fat	48.7g
Cholesterol	245.0mg
Sodium	3327.1mg
Carbohydrates	96.8g
Protein	61.3g

Ingredients

2 tbsps butter
3 tbsps all-purpose flour
1 C. milk
1/4 tsp nutmeg
1 tsp salt
1/4 tsp ground black pepper
2 tbsps vegetable oil
1 small white onion, chopped
1 garlic clove, crushed
1/2 lb ground beef
1 lb ripe tomatoes, peeled, seeds removed, and chopped
1 lb uncooked lasagna noodles
1/2 lb sliced mozzarella cheese
1/2 lb thinly sliced ham, optional
2 oz. grated parmesan cheese
2 tsps oregano
2 tsps salt

Directions

1. Before you do anything, preheat the oven to 350 F.

2. Place a large saucepan over medium heat. Melt the butter in it. Stir in the nutmeg with a pinch of salt and pepper. Stir in the milk and cook them until it starts boiling. let it cook for 12 min to make the white sauce.

3. Place a large saucepan over medium high heat. Heat the vegetable oil in it. Cook in it the beef, onion and garlic for 8 min. Stir in the water with tomato and cook them for 6 to 8 min or until the sauce becomes thick.

4. Prepare the noodles according to the instructions on the package. Drain it and place 1/4 of it in the bottom of a grease casserole dish.

5. Spread over it 1/2 of the meat sauce then cover it with 1/4 of the noodles. Top it with half of the cheese and ham then repeat the process to make 2 more layers.

6. Pour the white sauce on top followed by the parmesan cheese and a pinch of oregano. Lay a piece of foil over the lasagna casserole to cover it.

7. Cook it in the oven for 22 min. Serve your lasagna hot. Enjoy.

Mexican
Lasagna Layers

Prep Time: 20 mins
Total Time: 1 hr 5 mins

Servings per Recipe: 10
Calories	750.5
Fat	8.7g
Cholesterol	31.7mg
Sodium	1085.6mg
Carbohydrates	28.1g
Protein	16.7g

Ingredients

1 lb lean ground beef
1 (16 oz.) cans refried black beans
1 C. black beans, rinsed and rained
1/2 C. frozen corn, thawed
1 jalapeno pepper, seeded and chopped
1 (1 oz.) envelope taco seasoning
1 (15 oz.) cans tomato sauce, divided
2 1/2 C. salsa
12 no-boil lasagna noodles

1 1/2 C. shredded reduced-fat Mexican cheese blend
1 1/2 C. shredded reduced-fat cheddar cheese
1 C. nonfat sour cream
1 medium ripe avocado, peeled and cubed
4 green onions, thinly sliced

Directions

1. Set your oven to 350 degrees F before doing anything else and grease a 13x9-inch baking dish. Heat a large skillet on medium heat and cook the beef till browned completely.
2. Drain the excess grease from the skillet.
3. Stir in the beans, corn, jalapeño, taco seasoning and 3/4 C. of the tomato sauce. In a bowl, mix together the salsa and remaining tomato sauce. In the bottom of the prepared baking dish, spread 1/4 C. of the mixture, followed by the 4 noodles, half of the meat sauce, 1 C. of the salsa mixture, 1/2 C. of the Mexican cheese blend and 1/2 C. of the cheddar cheese. Repeat the layers.
4. Top with the remaining noodles, salsa mixture and cheeses.
5. Cover and cook in the oven for about 45-50 minutes.
6. Remove from the oven and keep aside for about 10 minutes before cutting. Serve with a topping of the sour cream, avocado and onions.

TEX-MEX
Style Lasagna

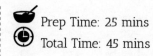

Prep Time: 25 mins
Total Time: 45 mins

Servings per Recipe: 5
Calories	447 kcal
Fat	24 g
Carbohydrates	33.2g
Protein	23.2 g
Cholesterol	79 mg
Sodium	899 mg

Ingredients

1 lb. lean ground beef
1 (1 oz.) package taco seasoning mix
1 (14 oz.) can peeled and diced
tomatoes with juice
10 (6 inch) corn tortillas

1 C. prepared salsa
1/2 C. shredded Colby cheese

Directions

1. Set your oven to 350 degrees F before doing anything else.
2. Heat a large skillet on medium-high heat and cook the beef till browned completely.
3. Stir in the taco seasoning and tomatoes.
4. In the bottom of a 13x9-inch baking dish, arrange half of the tortillas evenly.
5. Place the beef mixture over the tortillas evenly.
6. Place the remaining tortillas over the beef mixture and top with the salsa, followed by the cheese.
7. Cook in the oven for about 20-30 minutes.

Lasagna Caprese

🥣 Prep Time: 20 mins
🕐 Total Time: 45 mins

Servings per Recipe: 4
Calories   732.6
Fat   42.1g
Cholesterol   138.9mg
Sodium   1063.2mg
Carbohydrates   50.8g
Protein   39.1g

Ingredients

3 C. cooked and shredded chicken
1 (14 oz.) cans artichoke hearts, drained, chopped
1 (8 oz.) packages shredded mozzarella cheese
1/2 C. grated Parmesan cheese
1/2 C. sun-dried tomato, chopped and drained

1.5 (8 oz.) packages low-fat cream cheese
1 C. half-and-half
1 tsp minced garlic
1/4 C. basil, chopped
12 lasagna noodles, cooked
12 slices whole milk mozzarella

Directions

1. Set your oven to 350 degrees F before doing anything else.
2. In a bowl, add the chicken, tomatoes, artichokes, half of the basil 1 C. grated Parmesan and mozzarella and mix well.
3. In another bowl, add the half-and-half, cream cheese and garlic and with an electric mixer, beat until blended nicely.
4. Add half of the basil and gently, stir to combine.
5. Add half of the cream cheese mixture in the bowl of the chicken mixture and mix well.
6. In the bottom of a 9x13-inch baking dish, place half of the remaining cream cheese mixture evenly.
7. Arrange 3 lasagna noodles over the cream cheese mixture, followed by 1/3 of the chicken mixture.
8. Repeat the noodles and chicken mixture layers twice, ending with a noodle layer.
9. Place remaining half of the cream cheese mixture on top evenly.
10. Now, arrange the mozzarella slices over the cream cheese mixture in 3 rows, followed by the shredded mozzarella and basil. Cook in the oven for about 25 minute.
11. Remove from the oven and cut into desired sized slices. Enjoy hot.

WEEKNIGHT
Mushroom
Lasagna

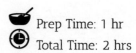 Prep Time: 1 hr
Total Time: 2 hrs

Servings per Recipe: 12
Calories	282.0
Fat	15.4g
Cholesterol	52.4mg
Sodium	533.4mg
Carbohydrates	21.6g
Protein	15.0g

Ingredients

5 tbsp butter, divided
16 oz. sliced mushrooms
3/4 C. onion, chopped
3 garlic cloves, minced
10 oz. frozen chopped spinach, thawed, squeezed dry
1/2 tsp pepper
1/2 tsp salt
10 lasagna noodles, cooked
1/4 C. flour
1 1/2 C. chicken broth

1 C. low-fat milk
1 tsp dried thyme
1/2 tsp dried basil
1/2 lb. Havarti cheese, shredded
7 oz. gouda cheese, shredded

Directions

1. Before you do anything, preheat the oven to 350 F.
2. Place a pan over high heat. Heat in it the butter. Cook in it the mushroom for 6 min.
3. Stir in the garlic with onion. Cook them for 4 min. Stir in the spinach with a pinch of salt and pepper. Cook them for 6 min.
4. Place a heavy saucepan over medium heat. Heat in it 4 tbsp of butter. Mix in the flour and cook it until it becomes golden brown.
5. Pour in the chicken broth while whisking them all the time followed by milk. Let them cook for 6 min until they become thick.
6. Turn off the heat then stir in the basil with thyme and half of the cheese until they melt to make the sauce.
7. Spread 1/2 C. of the milk sauce in a casserole dish. Top it with 5 noodles.
8. Spread over it half of the mushroom mixture followed by half of the remaining shredded cheese.

9. Repeat the process to make another layer ending with the milk sauce on top.

10. Lay a loose piece of foil over the pan to cover it. Place the pan in the oven and let them cook for 46 min.

11. Discard the foil and let it cook for another 16 min. Serve it warm.

12. Enjoy.

MUSHROOM
Lasagna

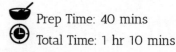

Prep Time: 40 mins
Total Time: 1 hr 10 mins

Servings per Recipe: 8
Calories	288.5
Fat	11.7g
Cholesterol	62.0mg
Sodium	814.3mg
Carbohydrates	31.1g
Protein	16.6g

Ingredients

9 -10 lasagna noodles, uncooked
1 (14 oz.) cans diced tomatoes with juice, undrained
1 (8 oz.) cans tomato sauce
1 (6 oz.) cans tomato paste
1 tbsp balsamic vinegar
1 tbsp dried basil
1 tsp dried oregano
1/2-1 tsp garlic powder

salt and pepper
2 C. shredded mozzarella cheese, divided
1 C. feta cheese, crumbled
1 (10 oz.) packages frozen chopped spinach, thawed and squeezed dry
1 egg, slightly beaten
1/2-1 lb. portabella mushroom, sliced

Directions

1. Before you do anything, preheat the oven to 350 F. Grease a casserole dish.
2. Prepare the noodles by following the instructions on the package.
3. Place a saucepan over medium heat. Combine in it the tomatoes (with juice), tomato sauce, tomato paste, vinegar and seasonings.
4. Bring them to a boil. Lower the heat and put on the lid. Let them cook for 22 to 26 min.
5. Pour 1/3 of the sauce into the greased pan and spread it in an even layer.
6. Cover it with 3 noodles sheets. Spread over them 1/2 of the cheese mix, 1/2 of the mushroom slices and 1/3 of the tomato sauce.
7. Repeat the process to make another layer ending with noodles and tomato sauce on top.
8. Sprinkle the mozzarella cheese over it. Lay a loose sheet of foil over the dish.
9. Place the lasagna in the oven and let it cook for 26 min.
10. Once the time is up, discard the foil and cook it for an extra 5 min. Serve it warm
11. Get a mixing bowl:
12. Enjoy.

Mexican "Lasagna"

🥣 Prep Time: 15 mins
🕐 Total Time: 50 mins

Servings per Recipe: 4
Calories	141.4
Fat	8.1g
Cholesterol	31.7mg
Sodium	698.6mg
Carbohydrates	7.4g
Protein	10.3g

Ingredients

12 -18 large pasta shells, cooked
1 lb. ground beef
3 tbsp taco seasoning
1/2 C water
1 onion, chopped
1 1/2 C. salsa, divided

1 C. grated cheese, divided
750 ml tomato sauce
chili powder
green onion

Directions

1. Heat a large skillet and cook the beef until no more pink.
2. Drain the grease from the skillet.
3. Stir in the onion, 1/2 C. of the salsa, 1/4 C. of the cheese, taco seasoning and water and remove from the heat.
4. In a bowl, add the tomato sauce, remaining salsa and chili powder and mix until well combined.
5. Stuff each pasta shell with beef mixture.
6. In the bottom of a 9x12-inch baking dish, place a thin layer of sauce mixture evenly.
7. Arrange stuffed shells over the sauce in a single layer and top with the remaining sauce evenly, followed by the remaining cheese and green onion.
8. Cover the baking dish and place in the freezer before cooking.
9. Remove from the freezer and defrost completely before cooking.
10. Set your oven to 350 degrees F.
11. Place the baking dish in the oven and cook for about 30 minutes.
12. Remove from the oven and top with the cheese evenly.
13. Cook in the oven for about 5 minutes.
14. Enjoy Warm.

FUTURISTIC
Zucchini Lasagna

 Prep Time: 30 mins

Total Time: 1 hr 30 mins

Servings per Recipe: 8

Calories	494 kcal
Fat	27.3 g
Carbohydrates	23.2g
Protein	41.3 g
Cholesterol	118 mg
Sodium	2200 mg

Ingredients

2 large zucchini
1 tbsp salt
1 lb ground beef
1 1/2 tsp ground black pepper
1 small green bell pepper, diced
1 onion, diced
1 C. tomato paste
1 (16 oz) can tomato sauce
1/4 C. red wine
2 tbsp chopped fresh basil
1 tbsp chopped fresh oregano

hot water as needed
1 egg
1 (15 oz) container low-fat ricotta cheese
2 tbsp chopped fresh parsley
1 (16 oz) package frozen chopped spinach, thawed and drained
1 lb fresh mushrooms, sliced
8 oz shredded mozzarella cheese
8 oz grated Parmesan cheese

Directions

1. Before you do anything preheat the oven to 325 F.
2. Cut the zucchinis lengthwise into thin slices. Season them with some salt. Place them in a sieve and let them drain.
3. Place a large pan over medium heat. Brown in it the beef with some salt and black pepper for 6 min. Stir in the onion with pepper. Cook them for 5 min.
4. Add the tomato paste, tomato sauce, wine, basil, and oregano. Cook them until they start boiling. Lower the heat and cook them for 22 min to make the beef sauce.
5. Get a mixing bowl: Mix the egg, ricotta, and parsley.
6. Pour 1/2 of the beef sauce in the bottom of a greased casserole dish. Top it with 1/2 the zucchini slices, 1/2 the ricotta mix, all the spinach, all the mushrooms and 1/2 the mozzarella cheese.
7. Top them with the rest of the beef sauce followed by the ricotta mix, mozzarella and parmesan cheese. Place a piece of foil over the lasagna.

8. Cook the lasagna in the oven for 47 min. Turn up the heat to 350 F. Cook the lasagna for an extra 16 min.
9. Allow the lasagna to rest for 6 min. Serve it warm.
10. Enjoy.

RAMEN
Lasagna

Prep Time: 10 mins
Total Time: 20 mins

Servings per Recipe: 4

Calories	698.6
Fat	41.9g
Cholesterol	253.4mg
Sodium	1670.9mg
Carbohydrates	36.5g
Protein	41.9g

Ingredients

2 (3 oz.) packages ramen noodles
1 lb ground beef
3 eggs
2 C. shredded cheese
1 tbsp minced onion

1 C. spaghetti sauce

Directions

1. Before you do anything preheat the oven to 325 F.
2. Place a large skillet over medium heat. Cook in it the beef with 1 seasoning packet and onion for 10 min.
3. Transfer the beef to a greased baking pan. Whisk the eggs and cook them in the same pan until they are done.
4. Top the beef with 1/2 C. of shredded cheese followed by the cooked eggs and another 1/2 C. of cheese.
5. Cook the ramen noodles according to the instructions on the package. Drain it and toss it with the spaghetti sauce.
6. Spread the mix all over the cheese layer. Top it with the remaining cheese. Cook it in the oven for 12 min. serve your lasagna warm.
7. Enjoy.

Pierogi Lasagna I

🥣 Prep Time: 15 mins
🕐 Total Time: 45 mins

Servings per Recipe: 4
Calories	1087.2
Fat	69.1g
Cholesterol	289.1mg
Sodium	1034.9mg
Carbohydrates	85.9g
Protein	31.1g

Ingredients

15 lasagna noodles
2 eggs
2 C. cheddar cheese, grated
2 C. mashed potatoes
pepper, to taste
garlic salt, to taste

onion powder, to taste
1 C. butter
1 onion, chopped
sour cream

Directions

1. Before you do anything, preheat the oven to 350 F. Grease a casserole dish with some butter.
2. Prepare the lasagna noodles by following the instructions on the package.
3. Get a large mixing bowl: Combine in it the potatoes, cheese, egg, and spices.
4. Place 1/3 of the noodles in the casserole then top it with half of the potato mix.
5. Lay another 1/3 of noodles on top followed by the remaining potato mix and noodles at the end.
6. Place a large skillet over medium heat. Heat in it the butter. Sauté in it the onion with a pinch of salt for 6 to 8 min.
7. Spread the onion over the noodles layer then cover the casserole with a piece of foil.
8. Bake the lasagna for 32 min. allow it to sit for 5 min then serve it warm.
9. Enjoy.

VELVEETA
Lasagna

Prep Time: 15 mins
Total Time: 1 hr 15 mins

Servings per Recipe: 1
Calories   5978.1
Fat   334.0g
Cholesterol   968.4mg
Sodium   8501.1mg
Carbohydrates   613.8g
Protein   149.2g

Ingredients

9 - 12 lasagna noodles
1 1/4 C. butter
4 medium onions, sliced
10 - 12 medium potatoes, peeled and cubed

1 dash salt and black pepper
1 (1 lb) box Velveeta cheese, cubed
grated parmesan cheese

Directions

1. Before you do anything, preheat the oven to 350 F. Grease a casserole dish with some butter.
2. Cook the lasagna noodles by following the instructions on the box.
3. Place a large pan over medium heat: Heat 1 stick of butter in it. Add the onion and cook it for 3 min.
4. Get a large mixing bowl: Press in it the potato until it become smooth.
5. Mix in the cheese, salt, pepper, and remaining butter.
6. Place 1/3 of the noodles in the casserole dish. Top it with 1/3 of the onion followed by 1/3 of the potato mixture.
7. Repeat the process to make more layers. Top the lasagna with cheese then cook it in the oven for 32 to 36 min. Serve it hot.
8. Enjoy.

Herbed
Greek Inspired Lasagna

🍲 Prep Time: 40 mins

🕐 Total Time: 1 hr 50 mins

Servings per Recipe: 8

Calories	670 kcal
Fat	42 g
Carbohydrates	31.2g
Protein	41.3 g
Cholesterol	189 mg
Sodium	2106 mg

Ingredients

1 (8 oz) package lasagna noodles
1/2 lb ground beef sausage
1/2 lb ground beef
1 clove garlic, minced
1 (28 oz) can diced tomatoes
1 (8 oz) can tomato sauce
1 tbsp dried parsley
1/2 tsp dried basil
1/2 tsp dried oregano
1 pinch white sugar

1 (16 oz) container sour cream
3 eggs, lightly beaten
3/4 C. grated Parmesan cheese
1/2 C. chopped pitted green olives
2 tsp salt
1/4 tsp ground black pepper
2 (12 oz) packages shredded mozzarella cheese, divided

Directions

1. Before you do anything preheat the oven to 375 F.
2. Cook the lasagna noodles according to the instructions on the package.
3. Place a large pan over medium heat. Brown in it the sausage, ground beef, and garlic for 10 min. Discard the grease.
4. Add the diced tomatoes, tomato sauce, parsley, basil, oregano, and sugar. Cook them until they start boiling over high heat.
5. Lower the heat and cook them for 32 min to make the sauce.
6. Get a mixing bowl: Combine in it the sour cream, eggs, Parmesan cheese, green olives, salt, black pepper, and 1/2 of the mozzarella cheese.
7. Pour some of the beef sauce in a greased casserole dish to make a thin layer. Top it with 1/3 of the lasagna noodles, 1/3 of the remaining meat sauce, 1/3 of the sour cream mix.
8. Repeat the process to make another 2 layers ending with mozzarella cheese on top. Cook the lasagna in the oven for 32 min. Serve it warm.
9. Enjoy.

FAMOUS
White lasagna Bites

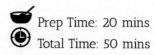

Prep Time: 20 mins
Total Time: 50 mins

Servings per Recipe: 12	
Calories	406 kcal
Fat	24.6 g
Carbohydrates	30g
Protein	14 g
Cholesterol	38 mg
Sodium	695 mg

Ingredients

2 skinless, boneless chicken breast halves, cubed
3 tbsp chopped onion
3 cloves garlic, minced
3 C. fresh spinach
1 1/2 C. ricotta cheese

1/2 C. grated Parmesan cheese
6 tbsp butter, softened
3 (10 oz) cans refrigerated crescent roll dough

Directions

1. Before you do anything preheat the oven to 325 F.
2. Place a large pan over medium heat. Heat a splash of oil in it. Add the onion with garlic and chicken. Cook them for 6 min. Add the spinach and cook them for 12 min.
3. Get a mixing bowl: Place in it the spinach and chicken mix to lose heat for a while. Add the ricotta cheese, Parmesan cheese, and butter. Stir them well until they become creamy.
4. Lay the crescent rolls on a floured working surface. Wet your hands and bring each two crescent rolls together to make a rectangular. Pinch them to keep them sealed to make 12 in total.
5. Place 1 tbsp of the filling to the middle of each rectangular. Pull the pastry corners on top and seal them shaping them into balls.
6. Transfer them to a lined baking pan. Cook them in the oven for 13 min. Serve them warm.
7. Enjoy.